Photographic Memories of

SHEFFIELD
10

C000257922

Broomhill - Crookes - Nether Green - Ranmoor - Fulwood - Crosspool - Sandygate and the Porter Valley

ACKNOWLEDGEMENTS

Many thanks to:

Michael Arksey and Eileen Cooke who contributed many of the photographs and information in this publication.

The Images from the collections in Sheffield Local Studies Library are identified by the Picture Sheffield number (e.g. s16484). Reproduced with kind permission.

Copyright 2008 © Michael Arksey and Eileen Cooke.
The rights of Michael Arksey and Eileen Cooke and their work has been asserted by them in accordance with the
Copyright, Design Patent Act 1988.
(pages 9-39, 42, 44-46, 48, 50, 70, 76-78)

Published by Arc Publishing and Print
166 Knowle Lane
Sheffield
S11 9SJ

Telephone 07809 172872

INTRODUCTION

Michael Arksey was a professional photographer who worked for Sheffield Photo Co. on Norfolk Row prior to opening his own photographic shop on Oakbrook Road, Nether Green.

One of the services he offered was the restoration of old photographs. Customers brought in their old, often damaged photographs and gave him permission to take a copy himself. Some were good photographs, some were old carte de visite pictures that needed a lot of attention, as well as old postcards.

One amusing story is about a lady who brought in a photograph of her father wearing a trilby hat. She asked Michael to reproduce the picture and remove the hat. When he asked her the colour of her father's hair, she replied, "well you'll see that when you've taken his hat off".

Photographs on pages 9-14 were taken by Horace Wilfrid Cooke, who owned a watchmaker and jewellers shop on Fulwood Road. He later moved round the corner to Glossop Road when the Fulwood Road shops were demolished to make way for the re-development to the site.

Sir John Betjeman (1906-84) - poet and critic of architecture, praised the district of Broomhill, in Sheffield 10, for its Victorian buildings and the abundance of trees.

INDEX

The York Hotel on Fulwood Road at the junction of Glossop Road. Postmarked 1904.

s15991

Tram No.53 at the junction of Crookes Road and Whitham Road.

Crowds pack the pavements for the royal visit of King George VI & Queen Elizabeth.
The York Hotel is in the background.

s03439

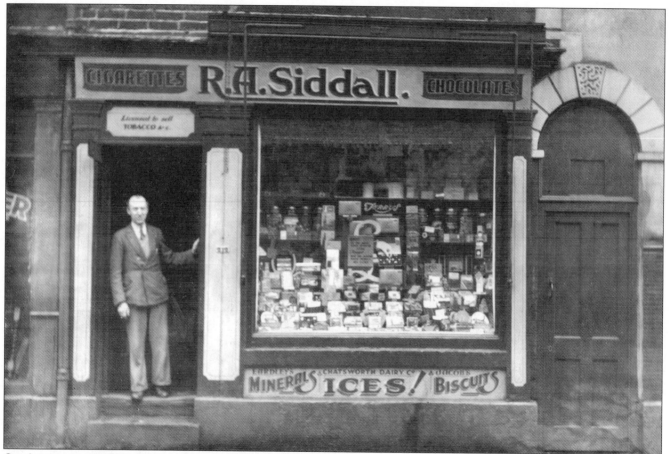

Confectioners shop R.A Siddall at 212 Fulwood Road.

s10555

The demolition of the houses at the junction of Fulwood Road and Crookes Road, c.1967.

The photographs were taken by Horace Cooke from the top floor of his shop on Fulwood Road, prior to his premises being demolished.

Spooner Road is the road going off to the left.

Fulwood Road before the demolition of the shops. Horace's shop is in the middle of the photograph.

Photo taken during the demolition. Nowadays I think the road would have been closed!

This house between the two shops on Glossop Road at Broomhill, was converted to a watchmaker and jewellers shop, after Horace Cooke's original shop on Fulwood Road was demolished. It is situated opposite Nile Street and the Broomhill Tavern

The junction of Fulwood Road, Nile Street, Whitham Road and Crookes Road. c.1967

South Sea Hotel on the corner of Fulwood Road and Crookes Road. 1967.

The junction of Fulwood Road and Taptonville Road showing the National Provincial Bank. Originally the bank was where Davy's shop is on Fulwood Road.

Nether Green

Hangingwater Road looking back to Oakbrook Road. A copy of this photograph was displayed in Michael Arksey's photographic shop on Oakbrook Road, when a lady came into the shop and said she was the baby in arms, in the doorway at the right of the picture.

Graham Road as it crosses Hangingwater Road.

The Co-operative Stores at the junction of Oakbrook road and Hangingwater Road. The tram to Fulwood is just leaving the junction.

An earlier tram coming along Oakbrook Road towards the junction with Hangingwater Road. c1905.

A similar shot but showing more shops on the left side of the picture.

Looking back up to the junction of Oakbrook Road and Hangingwater Road. The tram is one of the earlier ones.

A much earlier picture of Oakbrook Road before the co-operative store and other shops were built.

This shows the provision shop on Oakbrook Road. It has had several owners. H.W Peacock was the owner when this photograph was taken. The first name on the shop was Etches, followed by Peacock. Later owners included Barker, Bush, Shepherd and Oxley. The present owner who took over in 2007 is Andrew Green.

Bells shop can be seen in the previous picture, but here is a different view of it with some of its wares on display.

Tom Lane at Nether Green. The cottages are still there and can be seen about three quarters of the way up Tom Lane, opposite the junction with Belgrave Road. They have not been altered structurally apart from there being no foliage on the front of the buildings.

This horse and cart was photographed in the Porter Valley, exact location not known.

Hunters Bar taken looking down Ecclesall Road. 1884. The stone posts have been re-sited as near as possible to the original position. The photographer would have stood on the site of the old Hunter House Hotel.

A close up of the previous picture. The original picture was a very large glossy one loaned to Michael Arksey by the owner. He took a close up as the people in it were so interesting. 1884.

Hunters Bar. This was taken looking up Ecclesall Road, standing somewhere near where the Alms Houses now stand.

Boys in Endcliffe Park. Photograph taken on a lantern slide by T.G Hillman a member of the Sheffield Photographic Society. c1906.

The stepping stones in Endcliffe Park, close to the recreation ground. You can see the old bandstand in the background.

Rustlings Road from the junction with Oakbrook Road. Bingham Park is behind these houses.

The entrance to Bingham Park at the junction of Rustlings Road and Oakbrook Road. This is often referred to as Whiteley Woods, but old maps show the woods commence at Porter Bridge.

This picture of Fulney Road was taken from inside Bingham Park by the side of the Ibbotson Wheel Dam. There was a mill here between 1754 and 1902.

Westwood Road which overlooks the dam. This picture was taken from where Fulney Road goes off to the right.

Porter Glen (Hangingwater) - the junction of Carr Bank Lane and Hangingwater Road. Overlooking what are now the allotments that go down to Porter Brook.

This farm was on the southside of the River Porter, opposite Shepherd Wheel.

Waterfall in Whiteley Woods, close to Armchair Bridge in the background. 1906.

This photograph is named as Whiteley Wood Dam (Wire Mill Dam). The trees seem very close to the dam wall!

Whiteley Wood Cottages (Ivy Cottages). These cottages are close to Wire Mill Dam, off Whiteley Wood Road

BOLSOVER'S COTTAGE WORK SHOP,
WHITELEY WOODS, SHEFFIELD

A different view of the previous cottages. This end cottage was Thomas Bolsover's workshop. (The inventor of Sheffield Plate)

SKATING. WHITELEY WOODS.

Making a skating track on Wire Mill Dam. c1910

s04025

Old forge and workshops
(also known as
Whiteley Wood Forge)
Forge Dam.

w00174

The Refreshment Rooms in Whiteley Woods next to Forge dam, a popular venue for walkers and families who visit the children's playground nearby.

FORGE DAM WHITELEY, SHEFFIELD.   s04014

OLD FORGE DAM, WHITELEY WOODS, SHEFFIELD.   348.

Early 1900s photograph of Forge Dam Boating Lake (also known as Whiteley Wood Forge).   y01973

The last bus to Ranmoor. One of the ladies in the coach is thought to be Mrs Tregenza. A lady who knew the family came into Michael Arksey's shop and identified her. 1901.

Ranmoor church.

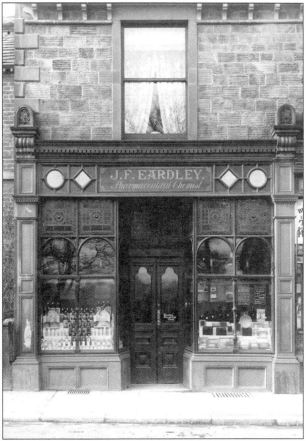

Ranmoor Pharmacy at 382 Fulwood road. s00843

These shops are just past the Bulls Head public house on Fulwood Road at Ranmoor.

Collection of carriages outside the Ranmoor Inn on Fulwood Road. Ranmoor Road is on the right of the picture.

Crosspool

Sandygate Road - Crosspool. Looking up from Manchester Road to the junction of Watt Lane and Sandygate Road. Shops now stand on each side of the road. 1919.

A later photograph of Sandygate Road with shops to the right, looking towards Manchester Road. s19362

Manchester Road looking back down the road towards Broomhill. A fine example of Betjeman's leafy suburb.

The old Crosspool Tavern on Manchester Road.

These shops were on Manchester Road near the junction with Lydgate Lane. One of the shops was
Arthur Ashmore & sons, Butchers. Note the concrete telephone box in the distance at the junction
with Lydgate Lane.

s17765

Manchester Road looking towards the junction of Stephen Hill. The Sportsmans Inn is on the left. The white washed cottage on the right was formerly used for Methodist meetings.

s19696

53

Sandygate

Cottages at Sandygate Road opposite the top of Pitchford Lane. 1910-1925 (now demolished)

s19257

The old Plough Inn on Sandygate Road. The carved stone over the doorway was dated 1695. It was demolished in 1929.

s06991

Lydgate

Both pictures are of Lydgate Lane at the junction of Tapton Hill Road. Note Bly's Blacksmith shop with the wheels leaning against the wall.

s09720

s17690

This later photo has Lydgate School in the background.

Old Grindstone Inn, from the junction of Lydgate Lane.

s00471

Crookes

Tram travelling along Crookes. Crookes Post Office and tram tracks leading to Pickmere
Road Tram Depot on the right. Crookes Endowed School is on the left.

s14630

Bottom of Crookes and Mulehouse Road. St. Thomas' church in the background. 1910.

Crookes Tram Terminus

Tram 225 at Crookes Tram Terminus. 1905 - 1908. Crookes Endowed School on the left.
Noah's Ark Public House is on the right.

s14806

Crookes Picture Palace. Opened 2nd November 1912 seating 660. Electric sound system installed in 1931. Closed in April 1960 and converted into a supermarket.

s02788

Cottages in Barker's yard off Crookes.
Situated between Toyne Street and Marsdon Road. Demolished 1908

s06201

Children out in there Sunday best. Photograph taken on Crookes, Springvale Road is on the left. c1900.   t02414

Queueing at 193 Crookes for provisions at the beginning of World War 1. 1914.

t02369

Crookes from the junction with
Stannington View Road (then named
Long Walk). Looking towards Toyne
Street and Rock Cottage. The group of
people in the background are stood at
the entrance to Court No.15.
The lady in the apron is Mrs Dale.
1905

s00729

Crookesmoor

BARBER ROAD, SHEFFIELD.

Barber Road at the corner of Burns Road. The drapers on the corner is No.32, stationers at No.34 and fruiterer at No.36.

s13255

R.A.F barrage balloon on
Crookesmoor Recreation
Ground, during the 2nd
World War

s03559

Junction of Burlington Street and Addy Street, Crookesmoor.

Tram No. 346 at Heavygate Road Terminus.

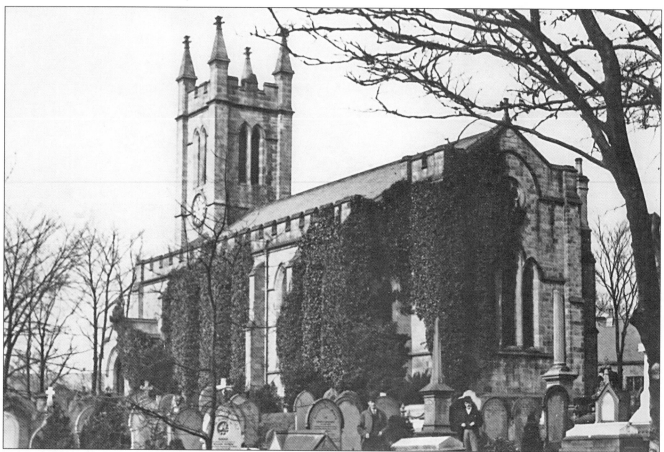

Fulwood Church from Fulwood Road.

Fulwood Coffee House, formerly the Blacksmith's Arms on Old Fulwood Road.

s06953

Fulwood Mother's Union on a Charabanc outing. The elderly lady in the centre still looks very Victorian but a younger lady at the back is wearing a cloche hat of the early 1920's.

s09155

Jeffery Green Cottages, junction of Brown Hills Lane and Harrison Lane, Mayfield Valley.

s06252

West Carr Cottages on David Lane, built in 1679. Mayfield Valley.

y02215

Lodge Moor

New Motor Bus Service, Lodge Moor, Sheffield. 2138.

Everyone is admiring the new bus at Lodge Moor Terminus.
This Daimler motor bus, No4 was in service between 1913 and 1923.
Photographed outside Lodge Moor Hospital Gatehouse, Redmires Road.

s16099

Lodge Moor Hospital entrance on Redmires Road.

Lodge Moor Hospital van parked in the grounds.

The Sheffield University from the rear, taken in Western Park by the Museum.

Western Bank. Children's Hospital is on the right at the junction with Clarkson Road. In the distance are the offices of J.G Graves Ltd, Westville.

s20425

Decorated arch on Glossop Road. Photographers getting ready for the royal visit of King Edward VII & Queen Alexandra. 1905.

v00475